Sometimes, in These Places

Rebecca Watkins

Thank you to the following publications in which
these poems have been published:

Anderbo Literary Magazine: "Searching"
Poetry in Performance Vol. 38: "After Baghdad"
Promethean Vol. 36: "Icarus's Daughter"
Promethean Vol. 39: "Remorse is an Infinite
Language" published under the title "What Happens
When You Mainline Fire?"
Red Mesa Review: "On Former Route 666"
SN Review: "Trinity Test Site," "On the Tuesday She
Turned 35," and "Reading to Helen."
Whiskey Island Review: "Verses"
Wild Age Press: "Irreversible"

To the many friends, colleagues, family members, and teachers who have inspired me and believed in my work along the way. There are too many of you to count, but I would like to especially thank my professors at the City College of New York: David Groff, Michelle Valladares, Elaine Equi, Marilyn Hacker and all my former poetry classmates for their feedback and inspiration including the River River poetry workshop; my Brooklyn poetry teacher, Joanna Fuhrman; Estha Weiner, A. Anupama, Juan Mobili, and Tanio McCallum for reading this manuscript in its various forms; and Mary Albertoli, Chaya Herman-Pilla, Kristin Reeder, Sharon Barefoot, Linda Kelly; my family; and my husband, Harry B. Sloofman.

Table of Contents

I.   1

Icarus's Daughter   3

After Baghdad   5

Prospect Street   7

Answer   9

Verses   11

When Night Was Day   13

Another Word for Repression   15

Remorse is an Infinite Language   17

Her Language   19

Christmas in Chinatown   21

Lazarus in Harlem   23

Hindsight   25

Horoscope   27

Forty   29

Being Broken   31

Isosceles   33

The Last Poet to Leave   35

One Year: A Sestina   37

It is Not My Intention to Confuse   39

II.   41

Sometimes, in These Places   43

Red Poppies   45

Waiting for the Fall   47

Morning Coffee, Neurosis, and the News   49

Thinking about Afghanistan on July 4   51

Another Suicide   53

Safety in Numbers   55

What Isn't Happening   57

On the Tuesday I Turned 35   59

Times Square   61

The Return of Persephone   63

Once Married   65

Her Name   67

The Third One   69

A Dog's Grief   71

Reading to Helen   73

Unsent Letter   75

Not an Apology   77

What Happened When Your Father Died?   79

This Modern Love   81

Irreversible   83

Good Matzo Ball Soup   85

Dear New York,   87

III.   91

Along Former Route 666   93

Thirst and Light   95

Someone Else's Penance   97

Trinity Test Site   99

The Way the Desert Loves   101

Searching   103

The Face of the Virgin is on a Taco in Amarillo
                                              105

About the Author   107

I.

Icarus's Daughter

I wore the Holy Ghost
like a sequined prom dress— stiff,
crinkling, and sweating. The priest
droned on about the Prodigal Son,
but I came from Icarus.

From the curved pew, I drifted
in dense silence, nascent words
caught in my throat like tight roses
waiting to bloom violently.

Inside me the fever for flight was born.
Hidden behind my face, doorways spoke,
a wire stretched tautly, singing in my brain
as I drank down the siren's wet song.

Sliding from strange sheets in the slant
of the morning sun, my wax
wings ran rivulets down my spine,
the beehives shook the honey out,
the world loosened its grip on me,
and Icarus's daughter fell.

After Baghdad,

she understood the reasons for hunger.
He, a PTSD fragment, gestated
in the living room and watched cable
until it was shut off.

He said he'd look for work
but didn't, just like he didn't
fill the prescription for Klonopin
because then he'd have to take Viagra too.

That's not to say they were experiencing
joy or chi in the bedroom, with the terrors,
the sweats, then one night he nearly
punched her in his sleep.

She watched her neighbors pull up
in a hybrid with their painfully
pink newborn, in its organic cotton onesie,
becoming green as the world around them
recessed on its haunches.

She thought about the drinks she hadn't
had since rehab five years ago,
and thought maybe a shot of Jack or Jim
would cure that hole burning through her
since he'd returned.

6

Prospect Street

After the raid the houses sat
empty. Then the workers came.
I heard their drills and hammers
each morning as I washed my face.

No drive-bys though, just rock and blow
on that street. Ten years ago, you could buy
the stuff downstairs through a slit in the door.

Sober now, a wife,
who remembers appointments,
notices weather,
kisses my husband good night,
prays against tomorrow.

Does he see my backward glance?
As if at any moment
something could bring it all down.

How I stood in that
current of relentless want,
bared my body and mind,
the way women do,
reaching for heat in all its forms.
Wanting to be murdered.
Wanting to be saved.

Answer

I meet her on the Greyhound bus
coming from Louisiana.
She chatters
toothless Bible babble,
favoring Old Testament.

I am a tapered girl,
nineteen with ribs poking out,
my smile peeling off
exposed and feeling dirty,
bumming cigarettes from strangers.

I get off the bus in Indiana,
never to see that old woman again,
but I remember what she said:
She said I am loved.

Verses

You will let me tangle you in my verses
because I have brought the colors that you need.

Later I will hold you
as you spit them back onto the floor.
I will lie beside you
and describe what worlds wait for us.

I will bring words and paper.
With this, I will twist out a cage,
where we will sit until we find
all the hidden ways out.

When you slip onto
that stained mattress,
I will watch your limbs quiver
with the basement horror of your dreams.

I will reach into your pockets
remove the bus schedules and matchbooks,
burn everything in your bathroom sink,
and crawl to lie beside you
only when I have destroyed all the evidence.

In the morning when I leave
I will hand you my knife,
(blade facing outward)

kiss your sweaty face,
hold your small frame,
and say please do not die today.

When Night Was Day

Hanging from fire escapes with burning throats
and blood in our noses, laughing into the
rust-colored sunrise.

Awake for three days,
we watched with reddened and stinging eyes
as the hygienic masses celebrated
an 8 am exodus. Clutching their lattes,
they boarded the Metro buses,
churning out bitter exhaust.

We said we'd spark riots with our poems,
spit paint into their blank eyes,
we'd sneak into their houses at night
and kill their TV's and eat their Bibles.

We were children of acid rain.
We felt like orphans
roaming in and out of bars,
sidewalks, bedrooms.

We may have cried,
but that's not how I remember it.

Another Word for Repression

When Sally Ride went to space,
I walked down Vine Street
holding my sister's hand.
We hid our fingertips in our fists
like teeth under pillows, tiptoeing
past the drunks sleeping on the sidewalk.

The year of Halley's Comet, my mom
took classes at the community college.
After school, we waited for Dad
at the Shell Gas Station. We ate Almond Joys
with the smell of gasoline in our noses.

When my sister took too many pills,
I hid my Barbie dolls under my eyelids.
I held my breath until I turned
sixteen and Danny Pearson showed me
how to get high using a Pepsi can.

The year I stopped drinking,
the birds fell from the sky as if I
were in an elevator going up.

I built a city under my bed
with the receipts from King Wok where
the Chinese woman said, "You always order
the egg drop soup," her black eyes

as cold as my mother's.

Yesterday, I took a photo
of the universe with my phone
and emailed it to Burt Reynolds.
He always reminded me of my dad.

Remorse is an Infinite Language

He leans in and says, "Cover your teeth,
the whites of your eyes, and toss that watch.
The magpies in Jersey are stealing everything.
They'll be in New York soon."

We float toward each other,
paper boats on rising water levels.
The roaming shoreline a hypothetical
backbone, one we would never use.

Subways rumble and hiss underneath us,
taxis edge into walls— yellow eels
sliding through bodies.

We strain toward suburban skies, as planes
crease the whiskey-colored clouds above us.

We swallowed flames, blind and stupid.
How else did we burn from the inside out?

He said we'd never leave each other out there.
He lied, especially about the magpies.
They were sated—they sang like goddesses
that year all over the East Coast.

Her Language

She didn't invent any of it,
she only noticed the ricocheting colors sizzling,
the dizzying speed of change and in noticing, she
brought it to life for him. Until his eyes
like two misty spheres reshaped themselves
to the contours of her world and his lips
to the contour of her shoulders.

Christmas in Chinatown

You bought wonton soup and a Buddha sitting high
on a thangka, painted umber and azure.
The steam from your hands
and our silent mouths entwined
above us, bleached branches growing.

I read the predictions about The Year of the Ox,
but that day I knew we'd never go anywhere
together. When the snow began to dot the darkness,
you walked ahead of me as if you could outrun it all:

the storefronts with tubs of swimming turtles,
the baskets of roots that looked like withered hands,
and the smell of fish that made us forget
        it was Christmas.

Lazarus in Harlem

*After "Dig, Lazarus, Dig!" by Nick Cave and
The Bad Seeds*

Lazarus was dead
face down, run over by a cab
on Amsterdam Avenue
when Jesus walked past him

hardly glanced at him
and his hazel eyes fluttered open
like moths' wings sheer and new.

Out I sprang from his chalky skull
like Athena from the head of Zeus.
Blistered by bone I made my escape,

tried to convince Jesus he gave
life to the wrong man, but he was already
down on 6th Street eating curry and naan.

When Mary (the virgin not the whore)
threw herself from the twenty-seventh
floor, on that day, Jesus became a man.

He lay down on a dirty bench,
wept, and got what it meant
to be in the wrong place at the right time.

23

Sometimes, I think I'm the cabdriver
who killed Lazarus, the immigrant, God's favorite.
When Laz took me to see Lady Liberty,

look, he said, the land of exiles;
but I was more of a stranger than he.
Then I slipped into the bathroom with

a gypsy and she read my mouth
like an open palm and told me
my life would be long like

a thread trailing from a sleeve.
She said I was made from his bones
and I could never leave.

Hindsight

I should have held him down when
I sang into his neck; heat would have risen,
bidden to dance or I should have wrapped him

lightly in my words, like gauze on skin,
a river that still rages under ice.
I should have whispered riddles into his back
while he slept, led him into frenzied dreams

and crossroads where I was the only oracle,
or I should have just walked away
that day when he held his hand out to mine,
his eyes glinting copper—the color of pennies,
the sun's prophecy burning the back of my neck.

Horoscope

Planetary alignments remind her that
now is an auspicious time to be alive,
to be alone, to keep the throb of desire
down and quiet. Forget the narcotics,
the smooth of a neck, instead, satiate
the mouth of the mind. All unpredictable
events will be found only on a white page
and not in words which fly from his lips to leave
an apocalypse burning in the kitchen.

Forty

He remembers how he made out with her,
on a velour couch, long before she was
his wife, his sneakers rubbing along
her calves after they drank pink wine,
fearing AIDS, loving English pop and
garage bands (or anything Seattle
with a goatee and flannel).
When whiskey still slid like ribbons
through his ribs, before he swore off
standing in grocery store aisles,
bathed and twitching in fluorescent lights,
love songs and granola choices overwhelming him,
before the vows, before the therapy,
before he ripped the canvases
from art school and wrapped them
like bandages around the days.
Before she shredded her poetry,
and fed it to the children,
but just enough so they all remained hungry.

Being Broken

I hold you in the outskirts,
in a place where blades of grass
have bent their backs,
and the night has rendered us

            to wild blindness,

a place where we can hear the rush
of trains moving
            like a thousand deft wings.

You say their urgency does not fool you.
You know there is nowhere left to go.

You tell me the light
is breaking you

            you've been broken before.

We are pennies left at the tracks,
the thundering
in our bones

            steel against steel.

The sky has stolen our children.

Their bodies shudder
symphonies.

Please don't wake them.
They dream like that,
in staccato motions.

Isosceles

I have been shaven at the edges-
becoming angular
becoming isosceles.

Did they bury the babies and the hipbones?
Did they slip the newspaper under my door?
Did mourning fingers scratch against paint, skin, and
religious woes?

What is the color of my lips
under the color lips should be?
What disease did I inherit
except the one I designed?

I have found safety in communication:
meaning, I starve less
when I speak,
when I throw out the estranged
request for help.

I watch the wind rise and dive into the concrete.
My jawline is inscribed with the chill,
I cannot recall who I was last winter.

The Last Poet to Leave

He waves one last time.
Buildings tower around him.

Rain smacks the concrete,
strikes his shoulders.

I beg the sun to emerge, erupt,
to nail him to the spot.

Don't let him leave.
Hold him there under August heat,

make him sweat with fever.
Make him fall in love

all over again with the stench,
the screech of the traffic,

and the girl he didn't
write a poem about.

One Year: A Sestina

She did not tell him about the fresh springs
that gurgled quietly behind her ribs.
She did not tell him about the vast smooth
of her mind or words their blunt red edges
popping bellies swelling in her throat;
the way the questions inside her grew.

The smoldering in the space between them grew.
On his bed, within weeks they tested springs.
His mouth on hers shut the fire down her throat.
His fingers touched her collarbone and ribs;
words scattered and dangled over the edge,
her shirt over her head his lips hot and smooth.

Soon the heat like a kiln glazed the path smooth,
the ease of the embrace and entrance grew.
Comfortable, she felt safe from those edges.
Weathermen promised a verdant spring.
Dogwood petals fell like bruises on ribs;
boughs bare and a ticking bomb in her throat.

He stared past her, something in his throat.
By August the river sat still and smooth.
Cliffs tore the sky like broken ribs.
Inside her walls tightened and tension grew.
Quiet like a kept animal about to spring;
she wanted to fly up to those edges.

Why did she long for the edge?
Why did he turn his mouth away from her throat?
The heat turned tepid, no longer a hot spring.
Both said they were fine, rocky made smooth.
Winter froze inside her; the space grew.
He covered her mouth with his words his ribs.

Like alchemy, snowflakes burst from her ribs.
If she stayed she would tumble from the edge.
As he slept, her pounding pulse grew.
Words became ragged ice and pierced her throat.
The road beyond the door beckoned and rose smooth,
but when he awoke they made plans for spring.

The walls were like ribs that held her until spring.
Fire grew and words flew from her throat.
She leapt from an uncertain edge; the fall was
    smooth.

It is Not My Intention to Confuse

The season swells blue and bright
against my door.
After too many months alone, I am
dizzy from the heat and honeysuckles
the bushes shaking
with scavenging bees.
I am dizzy with the thought of his mouth
the thought of my legs like vines around his hips.

But don't misunderstand; this is not a poem about
        summer and sex
or heat and wine.

It is just a poem about what rises off the cracked
        surface of grief

after time,
time and buckets full of mediocre days.

II.

42

Sometimes, in These Places

We push out of concrete—the spikes of grey
the scrape of sounds behind us,
across the bridge's glowing spine
over the darkening water.

In another place,
bark peels from sycamore trees;
a man paddles into the mist.
                        Silver minnows swirl while
                                hawks dive in
                        crumbling light.

Even farther,
a creek curves through the cord grass
                        like a strand of hair.
                                Does the air smell like
                        mud and salt?

Beyond the barren beaches,
            is everything
                shifting from light to dark?

Here,
people curl under slant roofs,
foreheads pressed together,
palms touching,
the day tucked into damp corners,

the dented garbage cans outside
chained together,
and the last taxi gone.

Red Poppies
After Poppies, Near Argenteuil,
Claude Monet, 1873

Just pick one. You've wanted to.
Feel the slender stem between your
finger and thumb, and tug. I am having

the dream again, not the one where
he turns from me but the one where
I am in the lecture hall.
I am teaching *The Odyssey* –the only
name I can pronounce is my own.

You have stood there in this field of poppies
for so long that the edges
of your dress are stained red.

In another dream,
the street is quiet, the public pool
empty and cracked.
It's so dark,
I can't see myself,
but I know I am running.

Just pick one; he won't be angry.
Place it behind your ear.
The world is waiting for you.

45

Waiting for the Fall

She waits for the leaves to spill.

Outside, the children make up a game
                          of running and falling down.

She's biting the jalapenos again
                          fighting back the melancholy.

                    It dances around her.

She stiffens; it is the lover she doesn't want,
spreading like spilled ink.
She tries to stop it crawling into her veins.

Why are they crying?
The children are falling.

                    Leaves burn into burgundy wisps.

A poem refuses to open,
balled up like a fist in her stomach.

She wants someone to sing into her,
                    so the lines of the poem

                          stretch out like fingers.

47

Morning Coffee, Neurosis, and the News

Friday:
Insomnia
German construction workers have migrated to
    Poland.
Together they are building a supermarket.
Two languages tumble against steel.
I watch my neighbor drag her garbage can to the curb.

Saturday:
Disassociation
Broadway stagehands are on strike.
Beware the tainted dog food and poisoned toys.
Remember to feed the meters.
I am gazing at the yellow tree.

Sunday:
Intimacy Issues
Persecuted Burmese monks march,
America is hung over.
America is at church.
Overhead clouds linger.

Monday:
Phantom limb
Politicians are trying to decide whether
    waterboarding is torture.
It's banned by the military, embraced by the CIA.

Today the sun enters Scorpio.

Tuesday:
Writer's Block
Sanctions are imposed on Iran's nuclear program.
I am no longer bohemian, wearer of watches, believer
    in twelve-steps.
Bukowski and Kerouac died drunks.

Wednesday:
Addiction
We are obsessed with the consumption of oil.
Finite resources argue, polar bears drown.
Suburban children wait for the school bus.

Thursday:
Co-dependency
Attraction is the impossible entrance.
Entranced by limb and mouth.
In Pakistan, lawyers are beaten by batons.
Here we claim our freedom after divorce.

Thinking about Afghanistan on July 4

Helicopters overhead,
cover their eyes with swirling black blades.

Women cradle loss in their hands
children blown into loose teeth and ribbons.

The helicopters' blades sing.

Fireworks blister the night sky.
Ashes rain on our foreheads,
Smudging our skin.

I watch the bloodless flag rise,

Unfurl.

An anthem of shame caught in my throat.

Somewhere, they await the blades.

Another Suicide

The River
I was the last one to slide up her ankles,
to wrap a wet hand around her thigh
to swallow her navel.

She stared into me as if
I am dangerous but

I kissed her broken mouth gently
like light rain on a windshield.

She had a choice.
I did not know her.

By the time we met,
her mind had split into rubies
behind dark crow eyes.

Her fingers fluttered like loose
wedding bells at her sides.

The Woman
A blaze of red needles pierced my eyes.

My breath caught,
as if remembering something good,
but before I could say the words

it was gone.

My body empty,
my bones just the shards
of a terracotta pot

that I, like a heavy blossom,
must have toppled from long ago.

I took off my sandals
and left them on the railing.

Safety in Numbers

The day the crocuses split their yellow
heads open, the beige couch smoldered
unnoticed during the family's lamb chop dinner,
until the alarm screamed and the dog
danced in circles at their legs.

They sprang up and yanked the spitting
couch onto the lawn while yelling at each other,
the dog, and their seven-year-old boy who spilled out
     after them.

They stood still like the naked birches,
staring as the couch crackled and withered,
the sudden hostage of a fiery hand.

Minutes later, two fire trucks sliced through the dark
and quickly, the men drenched the flames.
Patches of upholstery hung like tattered flags.

Afterwards, the boy, the dog, and the wife ambled,
bodies slack with relief, back into the house.
She cupped the boy's head, his hand on the back of
     her knee.

But the firemen and the husband stood outside
awhile longer. Their hands and jaw lines
glinted in the streetlight, and low laughter

and stories tumbled from their throats.

They talked like men who had known each other
for a long time, like men at ease because they pushed
something untamed back into the chest of the night.

What Isn't Happening

When my brother was in Iraq,
I lived on a farm.
I had dropped out.
I was yanking weeds

out of vegetable beds, trying to avoid
thinking
about death—
It was impossible.

A snake strangled itself in the netting
used to keep the rabbits out,
slithered through opening upon opening
until squeezed in a tight labyrinth of knots.

On the radio,
I heard the sirens,
2:10 a.m. Baghdad time.

The announcer said,
war had begun.

On the Tuesday I Turned 35

My sister called to say, "There are
tumors the size of Granny Smiths
on the walls of my uterus."

He paused the movie we were
watching and the actors caught
and held still, until I knew the scene
intimately. As I cried, he
rubbed two fingers up and down
my spine as if trying to smooth it out.

The next day as I drove, I saw
ice burst from the palisades
in frozen waterfalls and the lights
along the street glowed like orange peels
in glass. I crossed the Hudson River
and wondered what lived there in the shadows
of floating ice. What blood moved
coolly through their hearts?

Times Square

Look, we are in Times Square. I lived here
for a year when the photograph was taken.
Who took it, do you recall? On New Year's,

three sisters together for the long weekend.
Behind us leering at buildings, neon displays.
We smile but see that hint of an end, unspoken.

One of us married after the holidays,
and in the year to come, two lose men who
filled our time, one in kindness, one in rage.

Long distance phone conversations fill rooms.
By summer their names ceased being spoken.
By winter we forgot the specific wounds.

How long ago was that photo taken?
Your hair is shorter now, and mine longer.

The Return of Persephone

Persephone waits at the baggage claim reminding
    herself it's give
and take. She brought souvenirs from the underworld
    to give

to her sullen mother, who last year dismissed
the keychain and the coffee mug, saying her girl gives

in too easily to Hades. Persephone sighs. Every
May she must hurl herself down to be forgiven.

Every May she is shocked by the obscene petals;
she chokes on the fragrance the blossoms give.

Anyway, how can her mother ignore fate? Yes, she
    was young.
And there is the story of how his hand unfurled to
    give

three pomegranate seeds to trick her. Let them believe
what they want. Now this world above gives

too much glare, the autographs and the cameras'
    flash!
She imagines his fingers curled around her and she
    gives

into shivers. What she doesn't say is that she misses
    him.
The feel of grass is exotic, but the other world gives

too; it has taught her about darkness, how close it
is to light. Now she easily unfurls and gives

him her cool skin, and in turn Hades burns away
her questions. He says there is much he cannot give.

She replies, "It's overrated: the water, the birds, the
    sun."
"Then come back early," he says, and this she gives.

Once Married

Don't forget to cook the pages of your diary for
    dinner,
to slip your mind under your pillow at night,

pull out the map of your body for him to explore.
Don't sleep under the blanket of bones your mother
    weaved.

Don't let him know about the impossible burden,
or tell him that your grandmother broke a paintbrush
in half each time she found out she was pregnant.

Don't tell him that after each wedding anniversary
your mother curled a little more into herself like a
    leaf.

Don't tell him that you can't sleep
because there are birds living in the walls,

that your eyes are filling with forests, that you
are reading messages in the shampoo lather.
Don't tell him your life is moving over you like
    water.

Her Name

-for G. Lukens

Her name becomes a sound
muffled against flesh. A name
she relies on him to remember
because she begins to forget.
A name replaced with other words,
words that mean *need*.

The minutes she has alone
are intersections between
her blood and the tiny deaths
she feels with each birth.
She steals away to write
wedging her body between
her life and theirs.

The Third One

-for G. Lukens

He was the third one to die.
She didn't see him
but in her mind
he looks like the baby bird
they found last spring,
fallen out of its nest,
mouth permanently open,
its skeleton visible
under thin purple skin.

She stays in her bedroom lately
except to walk to St. Mary's Church.
Her hand moves over the backs of the pews,
numb fingers dip into the holy water.

She kneels and lights candles;
They said he wouldn't go to heaven,
this dead child of hers
his unbaptized soul lost.

She dreams of being cleaned
like the pumpkins
they turned into Jack O' Lanterns.

All the seeds and strings

pulled out of her; her face carved
into a frozen smile,
her insides burning
with the sting of empty.

A Dog's Grief

Sometimes, he remembers running, as
If he had no feet, smelling the fluttering
Of a familiar dusk, the slice of pigeons'
Wings penetrating his ears,
Renegade insects taunting him,
But that was before winter,
Before the woman with black
Hair went into lunar hiding,
Before the bird died,
When the house swelled
With hopeful waiting
And convalescence.
Then the illness
Came back with
The snow and
Took the man
Away.

Reading to Helen

Helen looks like she could be dead when she answers
    the door,
skin dry and folded, the color of nicotine.

Her face peers from above her long arms and neck,
blue eyes turned inward, blind, like two fish gone
    belly up.

In her apartment, the walls are made of books,
loose pages fluttering around us, brushing our faces.

We are covered with the sound of edges breathing.
Helen collects dead flowers; she presses each one

into a year until the decade is frozen in her gin.
This is how to make it smooth, she says, and sips
    from her glass.

Outside, shovels scrape against the sidewalk.
On the table is a photograph of her dead husband,

Past the window— the crush of snow.
Once she told me there was someone she had loved
    more.

Unsent Letter

The house fell sideways,
blinded in the shadows of our world flailing
on a busted axis, no one spoke again.

I wandered and found that cracks were really
canyons, and maps marked safety only led
to peril. My definitions were learned

in mirrors, reversed and unreal. Reaching
for you was always the dive, finding you
was the sudden scrape, my skin
torn against the rough wall of you.

I am the gardenias crushed on your concrete,
I am the banshee who screams
nightly from the branches of your tree.

Not an Apology

She grew up in a neighborhood where guns went off
and kids rode their bikes between bullets,
where crack queens jutted and pimps swaggered,
where teachers chose the ones they would save,
    those with straight A's.

They left and found a stone house between
two green hills, too sturdy to shake
when the people inside were crying.

She saw her father chop a copperhead snake in half,
a week later a turtle laid eggs in the yard.
She and her sisters hung clothes on the line,

and the shirts shook like ghosts in the cold
moonlight. All their periods came that year
and the loudest sounds were the moths buzzing
like traffic around the one street light. Her younger

brother learned to swim in the creek;
he didn't question the dark like she did,
having never known the way people
make the night a more manageable void.

She stopped praying during mass and meals,
tired of Jesus' gaping side and downcast eyes
while the country boys stapled Confederate flags

    to their walls
and fought to claim the next girl's virginity.

Nothing happened to her there that she would
tell the priest, nothing happened to her there that
she would write poetry about in college.

Nothing happened that could not be killed
by the whisper of vodka leaving the glass
and moving over it all like turpentine.

What Happened When Your Father Died?

Did time lurch forward like a boulder
from a mountain exposing the raw
earth where you left your daughters?

Did the lines on your face go hollow?
Did silence press you to its tremulous edge,
or were we always there like branches

entrenched in your bark? No matter
how far we spanned, no matter how far
you pushed, you still felt it when we snapped,

swayed, and were wrapped in chill.
What happened when your father died?

What sifted into your roots like compost
causing the dormant places to yawn open?

Did the naked sun blind you just enough
so that you finally had to reach out for us?

This Modern Love

The night splashes down
and paints the toenails of the fashionistas,
the foodies. They clutch their phones
like pistols cocked at the tyrant moon,
shooting any shadows that move,
sending text messages to ex-lovers
about fallow fields and dying.

On the corner, they're at again.
A stalemate —she won't say her mother's name,
or talk about the stain on the wall.
She won't tell him she kissed a girl in tenth grade,
a skinny girl with a crooked spine and flashcards.
They rubbed theorems up against
the chalkboard, they moaned out axioms.

She doesn't tell him that girl made her forget
the civil wars and the torn way
her parents leaned into each other
arms hanging in tatters, chests bandaged
to hold their broken hearts in.

Irreversible

Don't read after midnight.
You never want to wake up thinking.
Thinking is an irreversible act—
the beginning of a blistering bastard of a day.

Don't eat candy apples from the 7-11.
Don't keep your bee stings crying in a jar
just to remember how music feels.

Don't tell your therapist
that you are considering having sex
with the woman who built your cubicle again.
It's all part of your networking plan—
You kiss her with glossy business cards,
You grind against her like pumice.

Don't look as the world bites itself raw
around you. Pretend not to notice anything new.
Take twelve pills on Friday and only smile
on the Tuesdays marked in red.

But don't throw out the option of carving
your name in the elevator shaft
for those who are coming next.

Good Matzo Ball Soup

I came to New York only because he was the second
man to ask me to, and I had said no to L.A.
Not because the sketchy vegan scene on
    Venice Beach,
or the yogis and actors with their bleached teeth,
but because his daughter waited in Manhattan.

The days before the move, we made love with
 the windows open to the desert, let the moon
 splinter and soak our bodies until we became Gestalt,

a form greater than its parts. This, the last time
we were so open like fields turned and tilled
into one another. In New York, I was introduced

to his ex-wife and his guilt. I noticed how closely
his daughter's eyelashes resembled wheat,
her laugh a purer form than mine.

Suddenly it mattered that I did not know
good matzo ball soup, which was the local,
and which was the express, or what Soho means.

As I turned all those corners, the city winter sealed
itself inside my coat and I began to undo my love,
like unbraiding hair, like finding my way out.

Dear New York,

I had watched you for years
I knew you were out of my league,
but I said yes anyway. Like others before me,
    I fell.

I walked through the Village listening to the car
    horns, the crunch of tires on the asphalt, the
voices rising and melting into the air, my
    shoulders brushed against other
shoulders as I ate a slice of pizza dripping with
    red grease.

I got lost.
It was summer and
heat sprang from the streets
and blasted up my skirt,
but I was no Marilyn.

The next time I saw you,
we went out for lunch.
Then at the Met,
in the Asian Art Gallery,
we gazed into the face of Buddha together,
read about Kali's penchant for destruction,
and somewhere in the Ming Dynasty,
I began to relax.

I am ashamed to admit,
I gave in too easily—
the walk in Central Park,
and then later…

You were different than the others:
Cincinnati was so polite,
afraid to even bite my ear.
Albuquerque was always
talking about God and politics.
San Antonio was so aggressive
that I never had to make a move.

But you,
you lifted my hair from the back of my neck
and your lips found places
that the others couldn't even see.

New York,
It's been a while.
You are so busy and when you're drunk
you brag about all the celebrities you've known.

You smell like exhaust, piss, and grease,
there are rats playing on your train tracks;
they hop up on each other's backs like dogs.

At the subway station a woman begs for money.

She keeps asking, then apologizing,
"Please. I'm Sorry."
Her voice sounds like loose gravel in her throat.

As I walk up the ramp,
a musician sitting on a milk crate
strums his guitar and hums.
It's the same song as every Wednesday,
just a melody with no words.

I close my eyes and listen as it
echoes through the tunnel
and I am somewhere else,
back to the time when I first loved you.

III.

Along Former Route 666

In church, I watch as sand falls from the Navajo
man's boots next to me, imagine my legs around

him, my mouth buried in his shoulder
as we summon the old call.

Last night, I dreamed I was bargaining with
Napoleon, I did not want to fight,

only wanted the photographs of this
dead love he had stolen from me as I slept.

The Catholic brother asks us to pray,
says life is not so long, he does not

know that I heard the gesture of a raven's
wings. I held the sky in my mouth

thirsty and aching— I waited behind
the church gates for el milagro to come to me.

I drive south on the desert road surrounded
by eyes of the reservation. One eye sees

the story of a man and his son riding bare-backed
on a brown and white speckled horse,

a foal follows behind them. The other eye,
a trailer with tires on the roof while a boy and girl

circle outside like bees, their black hair flying.
Then, for miles there is nothing to see.

The earth is open, its dry bones exposed,
the soft luxury of skin gone. I rescue two hitchhikers

from a sandstorm, young white boys wearing white
        shirts
black ties black pants. They are sweating, ministering.

They ask me why I am in the desert.
Do I belong to a church? I reply,
Why try to convert me when no one can hear you?

Their glistening faces are like pieces of fruit,
ripe and unscathed. I want to lift my shirt,

show them the landscape of grief I carry with me.
I want them to dig their fingers into my ribcage,

pull the words of remorse out like a stillbirth.
They leave a pamphlet. On it is the face of Jesus,

his heart bleeding with the betrayal of thorns.
There are some roads no one can save us from.

Thirst and Light

I went to visit Louie
He made me Navajo tea;
Grandma[1] wound the clock
backward and the dead dog
out on the road stood
up and ran into a dust
cloud. The purple cacti
strained their heads upward.
The rattlesnakes rested
like burnt arms on the sand.
Louie told me whoever
it was had stopped slashing
the Puerto Rican nun's tires
after the medicine man
buried the fetish.[2]

---

[1] For the Navajos, any female elder is called Grandma out of respect.

[2] An object blessed and buried by a medicine man to protect or ward off evil.

Someone Else's Penance

I.

We pass the blowing black hair of the pilgrims
as they stream through the Sangre de Cristo
    Mountains
to arrive at the Spanish chapel, built on the spot
where two hundred years ago a friar knelt in the sand.

On that day he saw a light burning in the hills,
then pulled a feverish crucifix from the ground.

Now, people kneel and scoop the sacred sand into
plastic bags and small bottles. Letters and
    photographs,
taped to walls, flutter with testimony. Discarded
crutches, canes line the walls like the faithful.

I slip into the courtyard, among the clusters of
    novenas,
your whispered prayers flit through my ears
    while stars flicker
above like mica ground into the gums of the night.

II.

Two days later, after the prayers and the pow-wows,
after the scared sand of Chimayo, as we soak
in the hot springs in Ojo Caliente,
my chest falls open like a corset come unlaced,
water rises into my ears, mouth, and hair.

Beside you, underwater, I tear the words
from the deepest lines on my face, wishing I knew
if I am more my mother or my father.

Wishing I knew why I am jerked back
into a baptism of fear each time I drift my hands
over your body trying to know you.

Trinity Test Site [31]

Barren land stretches past all vision
Squat junipers clutch the sand,
their darkened berries dance.

Spires of rocks rise and mesas merge
with the alkaline flatlands, white sheets
whose edges press into the asphalt.

Ridges protrude like spines through skin.
Dry arroyos dip like the backs of knees.
In the land of Jornada del Muerto,

As the sun rose that day, the sand swallowed
our blinding dawn, the sky buffered our blistering
        kill, roll of fire.

The sleeves of smoke echoed over the face of the
        mountains
while sixty miles south in Alamogordo,
The Virgin was waiting in her rose draped altar

[31] The Trinity Test Site, located at White Sands Missile Range
in New Mexico, is where the first atomic bomb was
detonated on July 16, 1945.

for the flores and songs to protect the poor,
and the chiles were drying on the porches,
their bruised bodies swinging against the sun.

The Way the Desert Loves

I.
Stained with the blood of
reservation dogs,
her dry winds
scratch words into my skin.

I strip off my clothes and lie down
just to become one of her creases,

forgetting all other loves.
I cannot remember who I was,
who I hoped to become.

No warm waters of the womb here.
I crawl down her sandy spine.
It's a birth of the savage kind.

II.
I see no footprints in the sand but my own.
A yucca grabs my calf and leaves it
tingling like a sting.
I stand weighing my wishes against the sky.
Then I throw my poetry down,
the wind chases it into the canyon.

III.
A dream bruises my lips in the middle of the night.
I wake and go to the mirror.
I peer into the cities of my face
and see the chains that used to hold me.
I have lost time with bravery.
I am thirty; I am five
I am a woman and child:
an aging slip of flesh, laugh lines, and small breasts.
I hold my fire,
listening to it awaken.

Searching

I wanted to believe I was heard
that night I stopped driving
and leaned against the hood of my car
on Route 491 South between
Durango and Tohatchi.

I conversed with the stars
as if those swirling gases
light years away could convince
me my heart was more than
a galloping horse caught against my sternum,
moving me from one life to the next.

I had escaped from the desert
for a month and hid at an ashram
in the Rockies, feeling like it might snow in July.

There, a guru pressed her thumb into my
chest telling me to live from my center,
keep my intentions pure. Every day I chanted
Om Gam Ganapataye Namaha,
until the words worked their way
into my tissues and I heard them in my sleep.

I knew down in Roswell they believed in aliens
more than deities, the military swallowed
secrets with their morning coffee,

103

in the labs in Los Alamos scientists
blessed their bombs like babies.

As I drove back, I knew nothing more
than when I came. The moisture of the mountains
clung to my skin for one more day.
The desert sun roared against my forehead,
drying me out, pressing me to the earth as if trying
to break my body and reach inside.

The Face of the Virgin is on a Taco in Amarillo

She made a habit of stopping in Amarillo
    on her way east.
Eating a combo platter at Jorge's Bar and Grill,
she harangued the locals, while Hector, the waiter,
blessed her tortillas con queso with pluvial grace.

He was Catholic but she was born again New Age,
and quick to point out his platitudes were apocryphal
    at best.

Gurus are better than patron saints,
she'd rather follow the living than the dead;
    prayers are not mantras,
one is for begging and the other for breathing;
and a chinchilla is not something you drink.
She would know.

Back when she drank, she would have marched
Satan through the aperture of her skull
to silence the crows that lived there
eating the remnants of her belief.

About the Author

Rebecca Watkins has an M.F.A in Poetry from the City College of New York. She currently teaches literature, writing, and English as a Second Language at the college level and has created and led poetry workshops for all age groups in her community. She has been published in *Anderbo, The Promethean, The Red Mesa Review, and Poetry and Performance* among other literary journals. More of her work can be found at www.rebeccawatkinspoetry.com.

www.ingramcontent.com/pod-product-compliance
Lightning Source LLC
Chambersburg PA
CBHW030844090426
42737CB00009B/1109